In spite of fog

Journeying with St Julie Billiart

Sr Jane Hughes SND

kevin mayhew

First published in 2002 by KEVIN MAYHEW LTD
Buxhall, Stowmarket, Suffolk IP14 3BW
Email: info@kevinmayhewltd.com

Bible quotations are taken from the *New English Bible* by permission
from © Oxford University and Cambridge University Presses 1961, 1970.
Prayer to St Julie Billiart by permission, from *Be Mindful of Us*
by Anthony F. Chiffolo, copyright © 2000, Liguori Publications,
Liguori, MO 63057, USA. www.liguori.org.

Primary Sources
The Letters of St Julie Billiart
Translated and edited by Sr Frances Rosner and Sr Lucy Tinsley, SND.
Gregorian University Press, Rome, 1974.

The Memoirs of Mother Frances Blin de Bourdon, SND
Edited by Sr Mary Godfrey, Sr Julie McDonough and Sr Thérèse Sullivan,
SND. Christian Classics, INC. Westminster, Maryland, 1975.

Selected Letters of Mother St Joseph Blin de Bourdon
Translated and edited by Sr Mary Frances McCarthy, SND.
Christian Classics, INC. Westminster, Maryland, 1990.

Secondary Sources
To Heaven on Foot, private circulation, 1969. Sr Mary Linscott, SND.

This Excellent Heritage, private circulation, 1989. Sr Mary Linscott, SND.

The Life of the Blessed Julie Billiart.
Foundress of the Institute of Sisters of Notre Dame.
By a member of the same Society. London, Sands and Co., 1909.

9 8 7 6 5 4 3 2 1 0
ISBN 1 84003 874 3
Catalogue No 1500490

Cover design by Angela Selfe
Illustrations by Sr Joan Brown, SND
Edited by Elisabeth Bates
Printed and bound in Great Britain

Contents

My heart and my soul are at rest in my God through all the fogs of the Somme. God alone! An eternity without end is the prize of a little moment of confusion in this wretched life.

St Julie's letter to Françoise.
Amiens, 20 March 1808.

Foreword

The story of St Julie Billiart's life is that of a woman who, despite great suffering, never once doubted God's goodness to her. In characteristic style Julie belittled her 'dark night of the soul', comparing it to a journey that she must have made many times through the fog that often shrouded the River Somme.

In Spite of Fog seems an apt title for the story of her life, for Julie's faith and trust in God never wavered even when thwarted by state regulations or by Church dignitaries.

Her favourite expression, *'Ah, qu'il est bon, le bon Dieu'*, (Oh, how good God is!) became the motto of the Sisters of Notre Dame, the Congregation which Julie founded on the Cross and on her absolute trust in God's loving goodness.

Cuvilly

A Length of Material

One of my favourite places is a large department store which sells everything from thimbles to suites of furniture, not that I need to buy thimbles or chairs very often. The department I like best is the one that sells dressmaking materials. There I could stay for ages admiring the colours and patterns and feeling the different textures of the cloth on display. Sometimes, when I am there, I am reminded of a French girl, Julie Billiart, who lived in the eighteenth century and who worked for a while in her father's drapery store in Cuvilly, a little village near Picardy.

Julie's father, Jean François, owned the shop as well as a small plot of land where he grew vegetables for the family. The Billiarts had lived in Cuvilly for generations so he and his family were well known. At that time Cuvilly seemed a tranquil enough village, but for Jean François and his family this peaceful existence was not going to last. One morning when he opened his shop, he found it had been broken into during the night and most of his cloth had been stolen. It was not just a case of robbery: bales of material had been dragged into the yard and lay there torn and mud-stained and rolls of cloth had been thrown down into the well in the grounds. Obviously M. Billiart had an enemy who wanted to ruin him. In one night the whole drapery business had been destroyed and M. Billiart was now bankrupt.

You can imagine the effect this robbery had on the Billiart family. For some time business had not been doing well and there were outstanding bills to be paid. Now, land would have to be sold off to pay debts and any cloth still undamaged would have to be sold. The only problem was where to find a buyer. M. Billiart was in despair. He needed to find a market for his cloth but did not know where to turn. It was Julie who found a customer for him.

Julie was always practical. One of her sayings in later life was: 'Do what you can and don't waste time lamenting over what you can't do'. So, having prayed to 'the good God' for guidance, she put her plan into action. Early one morning she saddled the farm horse, carefully loaded the cloth onto the panniers and set off for the town of Beauvais about twenty miles from Cuvilly. It was a long ride for Julie and she felt rather anxious for she did not know the town or anyone who lived there. However, she put her trust in God and set out.

When she arrived at Beauvais, she rode through the streets until she found herself outside a draper's store. Once more she breathed a prayer for help and then entered the shop. God must have heard her prayer for the shopkeeper was an honest man who did not try to take advantage of a beginner to the trade. He listened sympathetically to her, carefully examined her cloth and then gave her a fair price.

As she returned home, Julie thanked God for his goodness to her. 'God has never failed those who trust in his goodness' was her strong belief and one which God had shown her at that time to be true. Now when I look at fabrics in my favourite store, I often think how much Julie would have loved to see, handle and perhaps even sell them. To me they are more than lengths of material: they remind me of Julie and are symbols of her trust in God.

Prayer

Dear Lord, there are times
    when I think nothing can help me
    and I have no one I can turn to.
At those times
    I become almost paralysed with despair.
Help me to remember, as Julie did,
    that you are always waiting for me
    to call on you.
Give me the courage to trust in your love.

Gospel Reflection

Luke 24:25-27; 30-32

'How dull you are!' he answered. 'How slow to believe all that the prophets said! Was the Messiah not bound to suffer thus before entering upon his glory?' Then he began with Moses and all the prophets, and explained to them the passages which referred to himself in every part of the scriptures.

And when he had sat down with them at table, he took bread and said the blessing; he broke the bread, and offered it to them. Then their eyes were opened, and they recognised him; and he vanished from their sight.

They said to one another, 'Did we not feel our hearts on fire as he talked with us on the road and explained the scriptures to us?'

I look around and wonder who on earth can help me.

Who can come to my aid?

Then I see, Lord, the hills that you have made.

Strong, majestic, towering above the plains,

they stand like fortresses.

To me they are a symbol of your power,

a symbol of your everlasting love.

You, Lord, are my tower of strength.

You will come to my aid,

will never allow me to be harmed.

Always vigilant,

you are my fortress and in you I find protection.

Save me, Lord, from all evils

and draw me ever closer to you in love.

Adapted from Psalm 120

Cuvilly

The Greatest Gift

A friend of mine is suffering from the illness known as ME. She has been ill now for so many months that at times she wonders if she will ever be well again. When I was thinking about her the other day, I was reminded of the illness which afflicted Julie when she was 23 years old.

To all appearances Julie's illness came upon her suddenly. One minute she seemed perfectly healthy, the next minute she was reduced to a state of helplessness. In actual fact, however, Julie's health had been gradually deteriorating as a result of stress and hard work. One evening, at the end of the day's work, Julie was sitting quietly beside her father in the cottage. Everything was peaceful. Julie sat sewing while her father read. Outside it was pitch black but indoors the oil lamp gave a comforting glow to the room. Soon it would be time to retire for the night. Suddenly the silence of the room was shattered. A stone hurtled violently through the window and a pistol shot rang out as a bullet was fired at M. Billiart. Luckily, the bullet missed its mark but Julie, though unwounded, was not so fortunate. The shock of the attack affected her whole nervous system. She tried to stand to escape from the room but found that her limbs no longer supported her. Sinking back into her chair, she felt a tremendous weakness and pain in every part of her body. From that time onwards, for twenty-two years, Julie was unable to walk without help.

In the eighteenth century many illnesses, especially nervous disorders, were not always identifiable or easily cured. In Julie's day, difficult cases, whether nervous or physical, were treated by bleeding the patient. In this way the doctors hoped to get rid of whatever impurities had caused the illness. Julie had been ill for seven years when an epidemic broke out in Cuvilly.

The doctor prescribed that all the victims of the epidemic should be bled and he decided that Julie should also be treated in this way. The result of the treatment was disastrous. Julie, already suffering from nervous disability, lost completely the power to walk. There were times when her body was wracked by violent convulsions and at times her power of speech failed.

Although Julie was unable to move without help, she was determined to continue some of the work she had done for the Church before she became ill. On the days when she was able to speak, she prepared children and adults for the sacraments. Parishioners came to her bedside for religious instruction and spiritual advice or simply to talk over their problems with her.

For a young woman who obviously wanted to do so much for God, Julie must have been tempted to think that she was useless. There were times during those twenty-two years when she felt that God did not listen to her. Perhaps it was during one of these times that she came to the realisation: 'God allows us to be deprived of his presence so that we may cling to him and not to his gifts'. Certainly, Julie through her illness had been deprived of precious gifts but her greatest gift remained despite everything else – her trust in the goodness of God. 'I go quietly day by day. I wait for the good God. I look at him. I follow him.'

Prayer

Thank you, Lord, for all the gifts you have given me and especially for the greatest gift of all – your unfailing love for me. I pray for all those who are suffering and in need of healing. May they find health, consolation and peace in your loving kindness.

Scripture Reflection

Romans 8:31-39

If God is on our side, who is against us? He did not spare his own Son, but gave him up for us all; and with this gift how can he fail to lavish upon us all he has to give? Who will be the accuser of God's chosen ones? It is God who pronounces acquittal; then who can condemn? It is Christ – Christ who died, and, more than that, was raised from the dead – who is at God's right hand, and indeed pleads our cause. Then what can separate us from the love of Christ? Can affliction or hardship? Can persecution, hunger, nakedness, peril, or the sword? 'We are being done to death for thy sake all day long,' as Scripture says; 'we have been treated like sheep for the slaughter,' and yet, in spite of all, overwhelming victory is ours through him who loved us. For I am convinced that there is nothing in death or life, in the realm of spirits or superhuman powers, in the world as it is or the world as it shall be, in the forces of the universe, in heights or depths – nothing in all creation that can separate us from the love of God in Christ Jesus our Lord.

When I think of your love, my God,

I am at a loss for words.

Your love gave me life

and renews it with every breath I breathe.

Your love, freely given, makes no demands on me

but only asks that I may love you in return.

No matter how often I change, your love never varies.

When I stray from you, your love calls me back

and has pity on me.

Every creature, every flower and tree will die

as I too will die.

But your love reaches beyond the limits of time to eternity

where you will love me still

and where I will praise and thank you for

your unchanging love.

Adapted from Psalm 102

Church, Cuvilly

Choices

Do you know people who cannot make up their minds? I thought of a friend who is like that when I saw a long queue of people in a department store waiting to exchange goods they had bought.

My friend is always doing that. It seems to me that she simply cannot make up her mind. At least that's what I think when I go shopping with her. Over and over again, I swear to myself that I will never ever help her to buy anything again. It takes her ages to reach a decision about the shoes, curtains or whatever else she is buying. In the end she does come to a decision but at the cost of my patience and, I think, of my sanity. Julie knew someone like that, perhaps even less decisive than my friend, for Julie wrote to her, 'Make up your own mind this time. Better mistakes than paralysis.' Thinking about Julie and decision-making reminded me of some of the decisions Julie had to make in her lifetime: decisions that would affect not only Julie but also a great many other people.

In order to gain control over religion, the revolutionary government in Paris had passed a law compelling all priests to take an oath of submission to the State. Julie, like everyone else in France, had to decide how she should respond to this attack on the Church. She thought of her friends now imprisoned who had refused to take the oath or who had spoken out against it: the parish priest of Cuvilly now in hiding, and sadder still, her friends, the Carmelite Sisters of Compiègne, who had been sent to the guillotine because they had refused to comply with the law. The Sisters had died bravely, singing the 'Salve Regina' as they mounted the scaffold. Julie had known them all well and at one time, before her illness, had hoped to join them in Carmel.

As Julie prayed for them and for the Church in France, the words of St Paul came into her mind: 'If God is for us, who can be against us?' When parishioners came to her for advice as to whether or not they should attend Mass said by the State-appointed priest, Julie's answer was firm and uncompromising. It would be wrong for them to take part in any of his services or join in his celebration of Mass. News of Julie's attitude reached the revolutionaries who were furious at her influence over the people. 'La Dévote', as they called her, was a traitor to France: she had harboured priests who remained loyal to the Pope, and now she was encouraging people to boycott the State clergy. Like the Carmelites she would have to be silenced.

In retrospect her decision may seem to us to have been an easy one to make; in the reality of her time it was not so simple. Julie knew that if she persisted in opposing the law, she would in all likelihood suffer a violent death and all those who listened to her and followed her advice would also be punished by exile, imprisonment or even death. No, her decision to speak out was made as a result of deep prayer and surrender to God's will.

In making her decisions, Julie was never foolhardy: she knew suffering and she knew what it was to be afraid but she also knew that God's loving goodness would be with her always. Later in her life, Julie was able to give the following advice from her own experience to a person who had to make an important decision and who was afraid of the consequences: 'Do not give way to fear. The good God is our strength.'

Prayer

Lord, help me in the choices and decisions
    I have to make today.
Help me to choose and
    act as you would wish me to do.
Guide all those
    who have important decisions to make
    so that they may do what is right
    according to your will.

Gospel Reflection

Matthew 22:15-21

Then the Pharisees went away and agreed on a plan to trap him in his own words. Some of their followers were sent to him in company with men of Herod's party. They said, 'Master, you are an honest man, we know; you teach in all honesty the way of life that God requires, truckling to no man, whoever he may be. Give us your ruling on this: are we or are we not permitted to pay taxes to the Roman Emperor?'

Jesus was aware of their malicious intention and said to them, 'You hypocrites! Why are you trying to catch me out? Show me the money in which the tax is paid.'

They handed him a silver piece. Jesus asked, 'Whose head is this, and whose inscription?' 'Caesar's,' they replied.

He said to them, 'Then pay Caesar what is due to Caesar, and pay God what is due to God.'

My God, I come before you in prayer

asking for your guidance.

I have always tried to do your will

and have not looked for honours or esteem

but only for your love.

Give me the strength to remain steadfast

to your teaching

and never to deny you

even if my life is threatened.

Never let me be cast away from you presence

with those who reject your love

or deny you for material gain.

Come to my aid, Lord, and guide me.

I love you above all things and seek only to proclaim

your goodness.

Adapted from Psalm 24

River at Compiègne

A Hay Cart

Driving along a country road for the sheer pleasure of it is for me absolute bliss, especially if I have time to stop and wonder at the beauty of fields, hills and trees. It is then that I want to join with the psalmist in praising God in his creation:

The ends of the earth stand in awe
at the sight of your wonders.
The lands of sunrise and sunset
you fill with your joy.

Many things in the country help to raise my mind to God: spring sowing and autumn harvesting recall Christ's parables; lambs remind me of Easter and the spotless Lamb of God. Even sheep, which make driving hazardous when they wander on to the road, remind me not only of the foolish things I do but also make me think of the Good Shepherd's constant love for me. But there is one thing that reminds me not so much of Our Lord but rather of heroic trust in God and that is a tractor-load of hay. Every time I see one I think of St Julie and of her faithfulness to the Church and its teaching in times of persecution.

It is frightening to think how violent the French revolutionaries were in their hatred of Julie who was, after all, a helpless invalid, unable to walk and at times unable to speak. She was not an aristocrat, had never been wealthy, and was now extremely poor. She could do nothing for herself and had to rely on the help of Félicité her 16-year-old niece, who had gone into hiding with her and who tried to care and provide for her by making and selling lace.

The hatred that had forced Julie to leave Cuvilly followed her to Gournay-sur-Aronde where once again Julie was accused of sheltering priests. The revolutionary mob knew that she was an invalid and unable to move so they made sick jokes about how they would toss her in a blanket and 'watch her dance' before burning her on a pyre they had made. Armed with flaming torches and shouting 'Death to La Dévote', they arrived at her lodging prepared to kill her but the house porter heard the mob arriving and warned Julie of the danger she was in. With Félicité's help he carried her out of the house and hid her in a hay cart that was standing in a nearby lane. As Julie lay there covered with hay, she heard the furious shouts of the crowd searching the house for her. When the revolutionaries had gone Julie and Félicité decided they had better leave the town to save not only their own lives but also the lives of their friends who were helping them.

As all roads leading to and from the town were blocked, escape seemed impossible until the farmer who owned the cart came to their rescue. At nightfall he set off in his hay cart with Félicité by his side and with Julie lying hidden in it under a load of hay. They left just in time for the mob had already gathered on the road to march to the house to kill Julie. Almost too terrified to breathe, Julie and her protectors passed through the crowd praying that God would help them. The farmer drove on as far as Compiègne and stopped in the courtyard of an inn where he abandoned his cart. He had to leave Julie in the cart overnight for no one could be trusted to give her shelter. When morning came, Félicité returned for Julie and brought her to safe lodgings that she had managed to find. For three years Julie and Félicité remained in Compiègne but during that time their lives were often in danger and five times they were forced to move to different lodgings to escape from the revolutionaries.

When I consider the state of Julie's health I can imagine how much she must have suffered from the jolting of the cart, from the cold, from exhaustion and from terror. I am reminded of Our Lord's words: 'The Son of Man has no place to lay his head.' In later years, Julie loved to tell people to have courage and to trust in God in times of difficulty: 'The good God loves you so much that he cannot let anything happen that is not for your good.' Her firm trust in God's goodness was her strength during this time of persecution.

God uses all manner of things to draw us to himself. He uses people like Julie and things like hay carts. As Julie herself said: 'Nothing happens by chance; it is always arranged by God.'

Prayer

Heavenly Father, it is easy for me to recognise you in all the glory of your creation when things are going well with me; it is much harder to see you in all the pain and suffering of the world when times are difficult. Help me to remain steadfast in my love for you just as your love for me never changes.

Gospel Reflection

Matthew 8:23-27

Jesus then got into the boat, and his disciples followed. All at once a great storm arose on the lake, till the waves were breaking right over the boat; but he went on sleeping. So they came and woke him up, crying: 'Save us, Lord; we are sinking!'

'Why are you such cowards?' he said; 'how little faith you have!' Then he stood up and rebuked the wind and the sea, and there was a dead calm.

The men were astonished at what had happened, and exclaimed, 'What sort of man is this? Even the wind and the sea obey him.'

I turn to you, God, in my need.

You are my creator and protector.

You provide me with shade from the blazing sun

and shelter me from raging storms and flood.

Save me now from the evils of war and revolution.

Like a snared animal,

I am surrounded by those who seek my life.

My Saviour, loosen the snare, save me from my enemies,

and shelter me as an eagle protects its young.

Your love gives me courage to proclaim your name

and call on you for aid.

You hear me and will come to my rescue.

My God, I trust in your abiding love

and praise your infinite goodness.

Adapted from Psalm 90

Hotel Blin, Amiens

First Impressions

Most people going for an interview try to create a favourable impression believing that first impressions are very important and that they are lasting. Only the other day I read that young people think good looks are more successful than qualifications in gaining employment and this made me wonder just how important first impressions really are. I thought of St Julie and the impression she made on people who spoke about her serenity and her smiling expression. But the first impression Julie made on Françoise Blin de Bourdon who later became her closest friend was anything but favourable.

In many respects, Françoise and Julie were so completely unlike one another that no one could ever have imagined they would become friends. Julie was the daughter of an impoverished draper whereas Françoise was the daughter of an aristocrat whose family owned estates in Amiens and Picardy. She was the grand-daughter of a wealthy baron and the daughter of a viscount and numbered among her friends the Madame Elizabeth of France, the sister of Louis XVI. Julie had been taught in a village school, Françoise had been educated at home by governesses and at convent schools directed by Benedictines and Ursulines. Yet in spite of such differences the two had a great deal in common. Like Julie, Françoise had also hoped to enter Carmel. Also like Julie, Françoise was hated by the revolutionaries not because of her religious beliefs but because of her noble birth. For this, Françoise had been imprisoned in Amiens; ironically enough, in a Carmelite Convent which the revolutionaries had commandeered to use as a prison. Whilst there, Françoise read in a national paper that she, her father and brother would be among the first to be guillotined when Robespierre came to the city. She spoke afterwards of the sorrow she felt at the thought that she would see her father and brother for the last time on the scaffold and told how she prayed earnestly for help at the time of her death. Her prayers were answered. Robespierre's reign of terror ended in 1794 with his own execution and Françoise and her family were free to return to their homes in Bourdon and Amiens. In the same year, Julie was invited to Amiens to live there with her niece in rooms owned by Mme Baudoin, a lady who used to visit Julie in Compiègne. Mme Baudoin was a close friend of Françoise and it was not long before she introduced Françoise to Julie. The first time Françoise visited Julie she was repelled by what she saw: a woman who could not move, who could scarcely speak and who needed to be fed, washed and clothed by her niece. It was only after repeated visits, and after Julie had made some recovery and was able to communicate that Françoise saw beneath Julie's physical weakness the depths of her spiritual strength. In time they became very close friends. Françoise told Julie of her spiritual longing to be a Carmelite sister and together they prayed to know God's will.

When Julie said years later to the first Sisters of Notre Dame, 'If we are not filled with the good God, we cannot let our fullness overflow into the hearts of those who come to us,' Françoise must have thought back to that first meeting with Julie and realised that had she judged Julie simply on her first impression and not allowed time for God's goodness overflowing in Julie's heart to touch hers, then they would never have really known one another or set out on their great venture of bringing souls to God.

Prayer

Help me, O Lord,
    not to judge others but to be
    kind and encouraging.
Comfort those who are ill
    or disabled and who have to rely
    on others to fulfil their needs.
Bless them
    and all those who care for them.

Gospel Reflection

John 1:43-46

The next day Jesus decided to leave for Galilee. He met Philip who, like Andrew and Peter, came from Bethsaida; and said to him, 'Follow me.'

Philip went to find Nathanael, and told him, 'We have met the man spoken of by Moses in the Law and by the prophets: it is Jesus, son of Joseph, from Nazareth.'

'Nazareth!' Nathanael exclaimed; 'can anything good come from Nazareth?'

Philip said, 'Come and see.'

No one, my God, knows me as you know me.
You know my every thought, word and deed,
everything that motivates me, every reaction I have,
my every feeling and sensation.
And this you know from before I was born.
I have no secrets from you.
You know me better than my closest friend
and love me with unchanging love.
Wherever I go, you are with me, loving me.
By day and night you care about me,
seeking only my good.
Help me, Lord, to love you in return.
Let me always be guided by your word.
Thank you for the gift of life
and for the greatest gift of all,
your abounding, unchanging love.

Adapted from Psalm 138

Amiens

A Birthday Cake

The lights in the little Italian restaurant suddenly dimmed and we were plunged into darkness. Then, amid cheers and the strains of 'Happy birthday to you!' a birthday cake ablaze with candles was carried triumphantly to a blushing 21-year-old. Everyone in the restaurant joined in the singing and shared in the happiness of the family. My friends and I sang along too although we did not know any of the party. We had simply decided to meet in the restaurant before going on to the theatre to see *Les Misérables*. Later that night after the performance, I lay awake thinking of France and the struggles of the poor and I could not help but think of Julie and Françoise, two Frenchwomen who had devoted their lives to working for the poor and the under-privileged and who celebrated a birthday, perhaps not with a cake but certainly with candles.

While Julie and Françoise were in Amiens, churches were once again opened and it was no longer treason to worship God. A group of priests called Fathers of the Faith began to organise missions so that people could once more be taught about God's love for them. These priests had hoped at one time to become Jesuits but were prevented from doing so when the Society of Jesus was banned from France. They had followed as closely as possible the rule of the Society and when the Jesuits were once more permitted to work in France, many of the priests joined the Society. Among them was Father Thomas who had celebrated Mass secretly for Julie and her friends and who had become her spiritual director. He introduced Julie to another priest, Father Varin, who believed that Julie had been called to do greater work for God than she was at present doing. He encouraged Julie and Françoise to invite others to join them and live with them as a religious community working for the Christian instruction of the poor.

On Candelmas Day 1804, in the presence of the Blessed Sacrament, Julie, Françoise and a young woman called Catherine Duchatel made or renewed their vows of chastity and promised, under the patronage of Our Lady, to devote their lives to the Christian instruction of girls. They also undertook to train teachers of religion who would go wherever they were needed. With the words of Simeon's prophecy echoing in their hearts, the three women promised to dedicate their lives so that others would come to know Christ, the light of the world. It was an appropriate feast for the birthday of the Congregation of Notre Dame.

Some years previously at Compiègne, Julie had been granted a vision of her future congregation gathered around the cross of Calvary and had heard the words, 'Behold the spiritual daughters whom I give to you in the Institute which will be marked by my Cross.' It is believed that Julie was then shown the suffering she would endure in her following of Christ. She must often have meditated on Simeon's words to Mary, 'And a sword will pierce your own soul too,' and prayed to Our Lady for strength to be faithful no matter what the future would bring.

The feast of Candlemas was once more significant in Julie's life. Two years after the birth of the Congregation, Julie and her sisters were reflecting on the prayer of Simeon when Julie was seen to rise in ecstasy, her face radiant. Tradition believes that God showed her that one day her sisters would go throughout the world carrying the light of Christ to those still in darkness. It is not surprising then that Julie chose 2 February, a feast celebrating both joy and sorrow, as the day on which she and her sisters dedicated themselves to the service of God in the congregation she called Notre Dame.

In the following year Julie took the name of St Ignatius for her religious name and Françoise took the name St Joseph for hers. Because of the strong anti-Jesuit feeling in France Julie was never called Sister St Ignace, but Françoise became known as Sister St Joseph.

Prayer

You, Lord, are our life and our light.
Renew in us the promise we made at Baptism
    to carry the light of Christ in our hearts.
Bless all those who are working
    to make your kingdom present
    to the poor and marginalised.
Inspire men and women
    with the desire to dedicate
    their lives to your service.

Gospel Reflection

Matthew 9:35-37

So Jesus went round all the towns and villages teaching in their synagogues, announcing the good news of the Kingdom, and curing every kind of ailment and disease. The sight of the people moved him to pity: they were like sheep without a shepherd, harassed and helpless; and he said to his disciples, 'The crop is heavy, but labourers are scarce; you must therefore beg the owner to send labourers to harvest his crop.'

As I watch the sparrows and martins building their
nests in the spring,
I think, Lord, of the home you have prepared for me
where I shall go one day to live with you for ever.
Your house must, indeed, be beautiful
for where you dwell there is love and peace.
I long with all my heart
to be with you when my life here is over.
Then I shall rejoice and be glad
and praise your goodness
with those I knew and loved
on earth.
Suffering and sorrow will be turned to joy and
you will bestow eternal blessings
on all who followed you in love.

Adapted from Psalm 84

Amiens

Walking

The other day I saw a jogger wearing a badge with the words 'Jogging for Health' printed on it and I wondered if the wearer was being sponsored for charity or if he was jogging to improve his own health. Then I thought of Julie and how, if she were alive today, she could easily have worn a badge with the words 'Walking for God' printed on it, for after twenty-three years of immobility Julie began to walk again and I think she must have become one of the greatest walkers of her time.

Julie's cure came about while the Fathers of the Faith were preaching their missions in the parishes of Amiens. They had the sisters to help them and all the community was involved. The young sisters instructed girls and children while Françoise and Julie instructed adults. Julie, because of her illness was unable to visit the parishes, but the people came to her bedside just as the parishioners of Cuvilly had done years before. Father Enfantin, one of the missionaries, became convinced, as Father Varin had been, that Julie would be able to do a great deal more for the Church if only she could walk. He came to her one day and told her he was very concerned about someone and asked her if she would join him in making a novena to the Sacred Heart for his intentions. Julie agreed to do so and began her novena that day. On the fifth day of the novena, Julie was sitting in the garden when Father Enfantin approached. He asked her as a sign of her faith to take one step in honour of the Sacred Heart. Without hesitation, Julie stood up and walked one step. She knew immediately that she had been cured but agreed to keep her cure a secret until the nine days of the novena had ended. On the morning her novena ended, Julie remained in chapel after the sisters had gone to breakfast, then she made her way unaided past the children's dining room to the sisters' refectory. The squeals of delight and surprise from the children who saw her walking for the first time brought the sisters running out to see what the noise was about. They could only stare in amazement as Julie entered the room with the words of the *Te Deum*, 'We praise you, O God' as a greeting. I like to think of the delight of the sisters and the children as they returned to the chapel to give thanks to God with Julie's favourite words, 'How good God is!' After her cure the Fathers of the Faith asked Julie to accompany them to the towns of Abbeville and St Valéry where they had been asked to preach missions. Julie went with them and wrote to the sisters in Amiens telling them about her work and also of a great joy she experienced. 'Today I had a happiness I have been deprived of for twenty-three years: that of assisting at Mass in the parish church.'

What we tend to take for granted Julie saw as a great blessing – being able to join with the people she loved in the greatest act of worship. Julie wrote many letters to her sisters, for no matter where her work took her or however busy she was, she always found time to write to them giving her news, inquiring about their welfare and encouraging them in times of difficulty.

In one of her letters describing the missions, Julie wrote of the surprise of some nuns in Abbeville who were much astonished to see her trot about. Yet, while Julie was in St Valéry, her cure had been called into question. While she was walking in the street one day, Julie swerved to avoid some horses and twisted her ankle so badly that she was hardly able to walk. Her companions, thinking her illness had returned and that her cure had not been genuine, began to make plans for her return to Amiens but Julie knew that God had other plans for her. With great difficulty she dragged herself to the nearest church and prayed before the Blessed Sacrament for several hours. When her prayer was ended, she left the church completely cured. From that time onwards, Julie walked countless miles in her zeal to make God's goodness known. She would have been proud and happy to have worn a badge with the words 'Walking for God' written on it.

Prayer

Bless, Lord,
>   all those who are disabled
>   in any way and
>   bless all those who
>   care for them.
Bless those who help us
>   to bear our sorrows and
>   help us never to take
>   their love and care
>   and understanding
>   for granted.

Gospel Reflection

John 16:23; 17:18-21

I tell you, if you ask the Father for anything in my name, he will give it to you.

As thou hast sent me into the world, I have sent them into the world, and for their sake I now consecrate myself, that they too may be consecrated by the truth.

But it is not for these alone that I pray, but for those also who through their words put their faith in me; may they all be one: as thou, Father, in me, and I in thee, so also may they be one in us, that the world may believe that thou didst send me.

A song of joy, a symphony of praise.

Would I had the skill to celebrate God's glory

and his power

with music and with verse!

God's word is life, is joy and love.

And we who listen to his voice are filled with peace.

Out of chaos beauty is created

and out of suffering joy.

Whoever trusts in his love finds

compassion and healing

and courage to walk in his ways

forever singing his praise.

How good you are God!

May your love be with us always

as we place all our trust in you.

Adapted from Psalm 32

Ghent

Opposition

The other day some of us were talking about all the changes we had experienced in our lives. First of all we spoke of what had been invented in our lifetimes. The list seemed never-ending because we were all older than we cared to admit. It was easy to mention television, computers, digital cameras and so on but it became harder when we talked about changes in lifestyles, in attitudes, in politics and in the Church. The lists began to turn into arguments for or against changes of one kind or another and it became clear that material innovations were easier to accept than spiritual or philosophical changes. Julie discovered this too in her day when her vision of a new religious congregation met with such great opposition that it almost destroyed all that she hoped to do to bring people to God. The Rector of the college in Amiens invited Julie to accompany him to Ghent in Belgium where the Fathers of the Faith had colleges. He introduced Julie to the Bishop there who asked if she would be willing to send sisters to work in his diocese. Julie agreed to do so provided that she had sisters who could speak Flemish so that they could teach there. The Bishop promised to find her suitable candidates and, true to his word, five young girls entered Notre Dame in the following month so that in 1807 Julie opened the first Notre Dame school in Belgium, at St Nicholas, in the diocese of Ghent. About this time Julie was also invited by the Bishop of Namur to visit him and discuss the possibility of opening schools in his diocese. Again, God willing, Julie promised that she would open a convent and school there in the following summer.

Everything seemed to be going exceedingly well for Julie and the new congregation of Notre Dame but this was soon to change. The physical sufferings Julie had endured both as an invalid and as an enemy of the Revolution were as nothing compared to the spiritual pain and sorrow she would now have to bear.

Before the Fathers of the Faith left Amiens they had appointed a young priest, Father de Sambucy, to be spiritual director of the sisters. Although he had no authority over the organisation of Notre Dame it was not long before he decided to make improvements to the Congregation. Unfortunately his vision of Notre Dame and Julie's were in complete opposition to one another. Julie and Françoise had founded a Congregation whose members would go out and work among the people, especially among the poor. They wanted their sisters to be free to go anywhere in the world to instruct people in the faith. They saw this as a special need of their time, for the Revolution had turned people away from the Church so that young people had grown up without hearing of God's great love for them. Father de Sambucy, on the other hand, could not accept the possibility of a different form of religious life from the long-established way of enclosed orders. He could not see that Julie needed to go out to the people instead of waiting for them to come to her. He believed the sisters should live a monastic life and not work outside the diocese of Amiens. He also wanted the sisters to close their poor schools and teach only the children from wealthy families. What he wanted, in fact, was to return to the way of life many religious had lived before the Revolution. The most important issue on which he disagreed with the foundresses was their insistence that all the convents of Notre Dame should be governed by a Superior General who would have authority over the whole congregation. As Mother General, Julie knew the need to visit all the convents in the Congregation while Father de Sambucy wanted no communication between the houses. So different were the aims of Julie and Father de Sambucy that within a very short time Father de Sambucy decided that Julie would have to be dismissed as Superior General of Notre Dame if the congregation he envisaged were to become a reality. Father de Sambucy was a very determined man who once he had made up his mind would not change it. As events proved, he would use everything in his power to achieve his aims and would not hesitate to manipulate others, even his bishop, to bring about what he wanted. The Bishop of Amiens, it was discovered later, had a serious brain illness which gave rise to mood changes and violent outbursts of temper. His unpredictable and inconsistent behaviour at that time did not make for a good working relationship with Julie and Françoise and they were unable to rely on him for the support they needed.

Father de Sambucy had been very strongly opposed to the opening of the convent at St Nicholas but had been powerless to stop it. Now he used the opening of Namur as an opportunity to get rid of Julie. She and Françoise had consulted with the Bishop and with his approval had drawn up a list of sisters who would open a convent and a school for the poor there. On the evening before their departure, Father de Sambucy arrived at the convent with a letter from the Bishop changing all their plans. The letter ordered Françoise to leave Amiens the next day and go to Namur to be the superior there instead of the sister already named. Julie was ordered to go with her and return from Namur via Bordeaux where she had been invited to receive members of another congregation into Notre Dame. Father de Sambucy demanded that before Françoise departed she should give him money which she had obtained from the sale of property she had owned, money which the foundresses had hoped to use to buy a larger house for their growing community. Instead, Father de Sambucy gave the money to another congregation of sisters in Amiens. He then insisted that while Françoise was in Namur he should have control of her income which he intended to use entirely for the house in Amiens. His actions left the foundresses without any financial support for the new poor schools in Namur or for any other work they would hope to do. They must have felt that their new congregation and their desire to work for the poor would never materialise, but Julie excused Father de Sambucy saying, 'His intentions are good. Leave all to God who can make all the events of life which to us seem most intolerable turn to his greater glory.' Without any time for leave-taking or preparation for their journey, Françoise and Julie set off for Namur. They were accompanied outside the convent by Father de Sambucy who, despite Julie's charitable interpretation of his actions, seemed to triumph in attaining what he had desired. His last words to Julie as she set out were: 'Mère Julie, you have finished your business here, you can now go and do it elsewhere.'

Prayer

Lord, give me the courage to be faithful to you,
    to give and not to count the cost,
    to fight and not to heed the wounds,
    to labour and to seek for no reward
    save that of knowing that I do your will.

Gospel Reflection

Matthew 5:43-44

You have learned that they were told, 'Love your neighbour, hate your enemy.' But what I tell you is this: Love your enemies and pray for your persecutors, only so can you be children of your heavenly Father.

Lord, when I am in danger I seek refuge with you.
In the face of so much opposition I feel helpless.
What can I do when so many are against me
seeking to destroy me?
How can I defend myself?
They destroy my reputation
and leave the work I have done in ruins.
What can I do?

Yet, Lord, you remain steadfast
in your goodness to me.
You hate all those who do evil.
Even should they triumph now,
in the end they will be brought low.
For you, Lord, love those who seek to do your will
and follow your commands.

Adapted from Psalm 10

Namur

Through the Fog

I was talking the other day to a child guidance worker who told me about a young girl called Kate who had grown up with the idea that her parents did not care for her but loved her younger sister, Marie, very much. They could not understand why Kate felt like this until one day with the help of a counsellor they remembered that just before Marie was born, Kate, aged 3, had to be rushed into hospital. When she returned home, the new baby had arrived leaving Kate to think that she had been sent away because her parents wanted Marie instead of her. For twelve years Kate felt unwanted. It was only when she was told about her illness coinciding with Marie's birth that relationships with her parents began to improve.

To be unwanted and dismissed by others is extremely difficult to bear. Julie knew this when she was turned away by some of her friends, dismissed by her spiritual directors and condemned by the Bishop and members of the clergy in Amiens. Yet, in spite of rumours and false accusations, she never complained or tried to justify herself. She wrote in a letter to Françoise at this time, 'My heart and my soul are at rest in my God through all the fogs of the Somme. An eternity without end is the prize of a little moment of confusion in this wretched life!'

When Julie and Françoise arrived in Namur, Bishop Pisani gave them a warm welcome in complete contrast to Father de Sambucy's blunt dismissal of them. Julie wrote to the sisters in Amiens telling them of the Bishop's great kindness and generosity in providing everything he could think of for their comfort, but she was obviously very concerned about the sisters she had left behind in Amiens because she wrote this letter at half-past three in the morning immediately after her arrival. In it she asked the sisters to reply by return of post. Their reply never reached her. Nor did they answer four other letters which she sent them about this time.

The only news Julie had of Amiens was given her by Father Leblanc who had been responsible for the convent in Amiens. He visited Julie and Françoise at Namur and told them that on the very day of their departure from Amiens, the Bishop had appointed Father de Sambucy to replace him. Father Leblanc pointed out that there was absolutely nothing he could do about the situation in Amiens because now he no longer had any authority there, and he added that Julie herself had none now either. He also told her that he believed all correspondence between Julie and Amiens passed through Father de Sambucy's hands and that the sisters had received none of her letters.

Meanwhile in Amiens Father de Sambucy appointed Sister Thérèse, a young sister who had been less than two years in religious life, to be superior of the convent. To mark her new status he told the sisters that from now on Sister Thérèse would be known as Mother Victoire. It was almost as if her new name celebrated a victory over Julie. As for Victoire, she found herself in a very difficult situation. She knew that she would have to obey Father de Sambucy by acting as superior but how, she wondered, could she possibly replace Julie or Françoise? How could she instruct the young sisters and novices when she had so very little knowledge of the spiritual life? She knew that she lacked Julie's ability to teach others and Françoise's quiet authority. Later these skills might develop but at the present time she felt incapable of acting as superior. Victoire told Father de Sambucy of her fears but he insisted that she should be superior and so she was left to cope with a task far beyond her powers.

Without the guidance of a spiritual director, Victoire devised her own way to gain sanctity. She spent long hours in prayer, practised severe penances and ate as little as possible. Soon the young sisters began to copy the superior with the result that many of them became very ill. She also took it upon herself to instruct the young sisters in religious knowledge despite the fact that her own knowledge of doctrine was limited. It was clear to the sisters that Victoire was not the right person to be a superior and they asked Father de Sambucy for Julie's return. It was only when the local clergy also asked for Julie's return that the Bishop wrote to Julie telling her to come back to Amiens as soon as possible.

Julie's return journey should have brought her great happiness but instead every stage of it was marked with pain: all her friends seemed to have turned against her. The foundress of the Sacred Heart sisters greeted her coldly as did Mme Leclerq, a friend from Amiens with whom Julie had planned to break her journey. In Paris the same thing happened when she called at the Sisters of Charity for hospitality. Handing her a letter which awaited her arrival, the Superior made it clear that the sisters wanted nothing more to do with her. The letter from the Bishop of Amiens showed that he had changed his mind for he now forbade her to return to Amiens or even to enter his diocese. After praying for guidance, Julie visited Father Varin to ask his advice but he too treated her severely. He told her of letters he had received from Father de Sambucy condemning her way of life. Now Julie knew why all her former friends had deserted her.

Mme Leclerq, Julie's friend, was the first to realise that Julie had been unjustly accused and, with the help of the Cathedral administrator, gained permission for Julie to return to Amiens although she was still forbidden to return to the convent there. Julie wrote to the Bishop asking pardon, as she put it, 'For whatever I have unknowingly done'. She was summoned to his presence and again asked his forgiveness. The Bishop told her he had nothing against her and wanted her to return immediately to Namur. Too ill and exhausted by the stress she had endured, Julie begged to be allowed to stay in the convent in Amiens until her health improved. Reluctantly, the Bishop gave his permission and Julie returned in secret to the convent she had founded and from which she had been dismissed by Father de Sambucy.

Prayer

Lord, comfort and console those who feel
    unloved and rejected.
Help them to open their hearts to you
    who love them with an everlasting love.
Forgive me for the times I have rejected others
    and give me the grace to see you in everyone I meet.

Gospel Reflection

Mark 8:31

For he was teaching his disciples, and telling them, 'The Son of
Man is now to be given up into the power of men, and they will
kill him.'

Lord, I am absolutely exhausted.

I have no strength left.

I cannot see where I should go or what I should do.

You know what I long to do

but am prevented from accomplishing.

Everything I do is criticised and condemned.

No matter how hard I try,

I am accused of behaving unjustly.

My friends have turned against me

and deserted me.

There is no one I can turn to,

no one to defend me against my accusers.

Lord, from the depths of my heart,

I call on you in my distress.

Be my saviour! Come to my aid!

Defend me and protect me!

You are my tower of strength.

With your help I shall remain steadfast.

Adapted from Psalm 37

Amiens Cathedral

Frustration

The other day I hurried around the supermarket collecting one or two items I needed. I was in a hurry because I had a meeting later in the evening. I headed to the express till – nine goods or less – and joined the queue. There I noticed with annoyance a lady in front of me with well over nine items waiting to be served. The next customer had two items without bar codes and so the queue was delayed until a runner was sent to find prices for the goods. Now there was only one person ahead of me and, of course, she had mislaid her credit card. I felt sorry for her but, to be honest, I felt sorrier for myself having to wait such a long time for only a few goods. Afterwards, I thought about my annoyance and realised how out of proportion I had allowed it to become.

We get frustrated about so many things: trains that don't run on time; buses that don't arrive; appointments that are changed with very little notice; repair men who fail to come at the time agreed. The list seems endless. Feelings of frustration come because no matter how we try there is absolutely nothing we can do to improve a situation.

St Julie in her day certainly experienced frustration but the way she coped with it was very different from our way: where we resort to anger or despair, Julie practised patience and told her sisters how she prayed to grow in patience. To us patience often seems to be a weak virtue. We think of Shakespeare's description, 'Like patience on a monument smiling at grief,' and think that patience is futile and lacking in energy, but Julie regarded patience as a source of strength: 'We need something more than courage; we need patience – great patience.' Julie wrote from her own experience, 'Souls of faith who put all their confidence in God and leave all to him will enjoy great tranquillity even in the midst of storms and squalls.'

When Julie returned to the convent in Amiens she was physically and emotionally worn out. Mgr Demandolx, the Bishop of Amiens, had given her permission to remain in his diocese only until her health improved but when she recovered she would be obliged to leave. Knowing that neither the Bishop nor Father de Sambucy wanted her in Amiens, she entered the convent secretly and withdrew to a part of the house that was seldom used. A few sisters were told of her return but word soon began to spread that Julie had come home and one by one the sisters made their way to her room to welcome her back. Victoire was one of the first to see her and impulsively offered to resign as superior but Julie very wisely declined her offer. She knew that Victoire was the person Father de Sambucy and the Bishop wanted to be in charge of the convent and that she herself was only there on sufferance. When Father de Sambucy heard Julie had returned, he was angry and lost no time in telling her that she would no longer be called 'Mère' Julie but would simply be addressed by the title 'Madame'. Once again it was the Bishop who altered things: the local clergy and the sisters had represented that Victoire was not capable of giving spiritual direction to the sisters and so, now that Julie was back in Amiens, he decided to reinstall her as Reverend Mother. Julie, knowing how often the Bishop changed his mind, must have wondered how long her position was likely to last. Father de Sambucy objected to her appointment, stating that Victoire's term of office for three years was still binding and proposed instead that Julie and Victoire should be co-superiors, an arrangement which Julie foresaw would cause difficulty in her relationships with Victoire as well as tension in the community. Meanwhile, the Bishop of Namur was so pleased with the work of the sisters in his diocese that he asked Julie if she would open a school for poor children in the town of Jumet. Mgr Demandolx approved of this new foundation and asked Julie to name the sisters who would go there. Having given the matter careful thought, Julie drew up a list of sisters and presented it to the Bishop for his approval, asking that she should travel with them to Jumet and see them settled in their new home. The Bishop gave his approval and all seemed well. Julie drew up the list of sisters with great consideration for Victoire. It was obvious that Victoire had felt slighted and humiliated when Julie had been reinstated as Reverend Mother and that she still felt rejected when the sisters turned to Julie for advice. Because of this Julie named Victoire as superior of the new convent hoping that a position of authority would help her regain some of the prestige she felt she had lost. Unfortunately, Julie had not considered how Father de Sambucy would react to her proposal. He lost no time in telling the Bishop that Julie was jealous of Victoire and was trying to get rid of her from Amiens. The Bishop believed him and withdrew permission for the sisters to go to Jumet until another list was drawn up, omitting Victoire's name. When this list was made, the sisters prepared once more to set out for Jumet. Once more the Bishop gave his permission but withdrew it again the following day. On two more occasions the Bishop gave his permission for the house at Jumet to be opened but each time withdrew his permission without any reason being given. Finally the Bishop agreed to let the sisters travel but forbade Julie to go with them. One can imagine how Julie must have felt. She wanted to provide religious education and schooling for poor children but instead found herself in a kind of cat-and-mouse situation. In a letter to Françoise Julie wrote, 'It is so extraordinary that they should behave like this towards me; first they had not wanted me within a hundred leagues of them, and now they will not let me take a step outside the house.' And in another letter about the same time, 'Here I am restricted without any liberty. There is nothing left to do. When the answer *no* has been given, nothing more is to be said. If this is the holy will of my God everything will go well, but if the good God wants things different he will know how to arrange them for the best. May the holy will of God be done in all of us. Let us stay firmly anchored there in all the events of our lives.'

Prayer

Lord Jesus Christ, you knew what it was to be frustrated in your desire to bring all people into the Kingdom of God. Give me the grace to be patient with others as you are patient with me.

Gospel Reflection

Mark 6:1-6

He left that place and went to his home town accompanied by his disciples. When the Sabbath came he began to teach in the synagogue; and the large congregation who heard him were amazed and said, 'Where does he get it from?' and, 'What wisdom is this that has been given him?' and, 'How does he work such miracles? Is not this the carpenter, the son of Mary, the brother of James and Joseph and Judas and Simon? And are not his sisters with us?' So they fell foul of him.

Jesus said to them, 'A prophet will always be held in honour except in his home town, and among his kinsmen and family.' He could work no miracle there, except that he put his hands on a few sick people and healed them; and he was taken aback by their want of faith.

Lord, my soul is at peace with you,
for in you I find comfort and strength.
Nothing can shake my confidence
in your loving goodness,
though people conspire against me
and seek to destroy me.
I seek only to do your will but stand accused of
envy, malice, self-interest and pride.
Those whom I look to for help no longer trust me.
But you, Lord, know me through and through
and you, my God and Saviour
will never desert me.
I place all my trust in you.

Adapted from Psalm 61

Jumet

Courage

In an article I read recently the word 'courage' was defined as 'facing danger with confidence and determination', and examples were given of famous people from fiction and real life who showed courage in their lives. I read through the list of names with interest. King David and Esther were alongside Beowulf and Martin Luther King. I noticed that St Teresa was also in the company because of her bravery in reforming the Carmelites despite the opposition of her ecclesiastical superiors. Her name made me think of St Julie who, two and a half centuries after Teresa, had to endure similar hostility.

After weeks of delay during which Mgr Demandolx hesitated to let the sisters go to Jumet, he finally gave his consent on condition that Julie should remain in Amiens and so two sisters set out to begin their apostolate in Belgium. They were full of enthusiasm for their new work but were a little sad at leaving Amiens and very disappointed that Julie had been forbidden to go with them. However, with missionary zeal they set out with confidence, a confidence that was soon to be put to the test.

Because of the procrastination about the date of their departure to Jumet, the parish there was unprepared for their arrival. There was also an added complication as the parish priest who had been involved in their coming to Jumet had been moved to another parish and had forgotten to leave any word about their arrival. When the sisters entered their new home, they were dismayed by its condition. The first thing they were aware of was the damp, unlived-in smell of the house. As they went from room to room they became even more discouraged. Moisture on the bare walls accounted for the clammy atmosphere. There was no furniture anywhere, not even beds which the sisters thought would have been provided. Instead there was only some straw lying in a heap on the floor. During their journey they had looked forward to having a warm meal on their arrival, but now they found there was no food anywhere in the house. They looked everywhere to find fuel of some kind to give light and heat but there was none to be found. Cold, tired and hungry, they said their night prayers together, thanked God for a safe journey and asked a blessing on their new mission in Jumet.

When the sisters wrote to Julie telling her of their safe arrival and of the dreadful conditions they were living in, she wished with all her heart that she had been allowed to travel to Jumet with them for she would never have allowed them to remain in such unhealthy conditions, but her hands were tied and there was nothing she could do except repeat her requests to go to Jumet.

Mgr Demandolx had been told of the sisters' circumstances and eventually spoke to Julie about them. He rebuked her smilingly saying that it was almost a mortal sin to send sisters to live in such a damp house and ordered her to go at once to Jumet to see if she could better their situation. By doing this, it seemed that he was making it clear that he and not Julie was responsible for the welfare of the sisters and that she did not have any authority as Superior General to visit the convents of her sisters.

Before Julie left for Jumet, some of the young sisters had stopped her at the last minute and asked whom they should consult for spiritual direction in her absence. Julie named the Mistress of Novices as the person most likely to help them and then set off on her journey. She was given a great welcome in Jumet and soon saw for herself the conditions the sisters had been writing about. As she sat and talked with them, they told her about the difficulties they experienced in their daily living and in their teaching and with her advice they planned changes to improve both their community arrangements and the organisation of their school.

Feeling happier about the sisters in Jumet, Julie left for Namur and met Françoise who planned to journey part of the way with her to Amiens. The Bishop of Namur had advised Françoise to return there and ask Father de Sambucy to give her back the control of her finances which he had taken over when she moved from Amiens.

On the journey back to Amiens, Julie received a devastating letter from Mgr Demandolx in which he condemned her disobedience, her pride and her sham humility and accused her of being jealous of Sister Victoire. The reason for this tirade was that Julie had named the novice mistress and not Victoire as the person who should help the young sisters in her absence.

Julie must have felt that there was nothing she could do that was right as far as the Bishop was concerned.

Instead of returning happily to Amiens, having seen to the sisters' needs in Jumet, Julie must have made her way back to Amiens wondering what awaited her there.

Prayer

Lord, bless all those who are working
   to bring about your Kingdom here on earth.
Give them the strength to persevere in spite of
   opposition and negative criticism.

Gospel Reflection

Luke 22:39-44

Then he went out and made his way as usual to the Mount of Olives, accompanied by his disciples. When he reached the place he said to them, 'Pray that you may be spared the hour of testing.' He himself withdrew from them about a stone's throw, knelt down, and began to pray: 'Father, if it be thy will, take this cup away from me. Yet not my will but thine be done.'

And now there appeared to him an angel from heaven bringing him strength, and in anguish of spirit he prayed the more urgently; and his sweat was like clots of blood falling to the ground.

When he rose from prayer and came to the disciples he found them asleep, worn out by grief. 'Why are you sleeping?' he said. 'Rise and pray that you may be spared the test.'

Lord, you are my Saviour,

I thank you for your goodness to me.

In the midst of my distress, I praise your holy name

and trust in you to rescue me.

You alone can judge me truly

for you alone know my innermost thoughts

and desires.

Lord, you hear the prayer of the poor.

Listen to me now, for I am poor and needy.

Never let me despair of your loving mercy.

Give me the courage to be steadfast to your teachings

and to walk bravely along the path you have chosen for me.

Adapted from Psalm 9

Amiens

Walking on Eggshells

Last week I had an interesting but disturbing chat with a lady whom I sat beside on a bus. We did not know each other and perhaps that is why she felt she could confide in me. After talking generally about the weather and television, she told me that she was hoping to change jobs and was looking forward to this very much. She worked in an office and found life there very difficult. No, she was not bullied, but was so exhausted in trying to keep the peace and not give cause for complaint or hurt feelings that she just wanted to move away. It was one person in particular, her immediate senior in the firm, who was so power-conscious that she took it as an insult if the boss overlooked her and spoke to my travelling companion first instead of to her. Not being a psychiatrist and not knowing the whole background to the story, I agreed with her that she must be finding life very stressful. Then she said something that made me think. She said, 'It's like walking on eggshells', and I knew exactly what she meant because sometimes I have that feeling myself when dealing with people.

Julie Billiart would certainly have known how my companion felt for she had to cope with angry and jealous people who opposed the good that she was trying to do. She was saddened by their critical and unkind remarks: she would not have been human had she not felt the pain and hurt. Instead of being resentful she turned to her good God in prayer. 'Let us stay calm,' she wrote to Françoise when she heard how people were talking unkindly about her, 'and it will be much easier to hear the good God . . . All kinds of noises do not reach my heart. Everything is astir, but I see the good God making use of it all.'

After reading the letter that Mgr Demandolx had sent her

in which he accused her of being disobedient, proud and jealous, Julie knew that she would not be received kindly when she returned to Amiens. Nor was she mistaken. The Bishop greeted her coldly and without wasting time told her that she would no longer be Superior General of the Sisters of Notre Dame. He also told her that there would be no need for a Superior General as each convent would now be completely independent of the others.

Julie listened quietly to what he had to say but was devastated by his decisions for this would mean the end of the congregation as she saw it. To Julie it was essential that there should be a Superior General in charge of the whole congregation even if she herself were not that person. A Superior General would be able to send the sisters wherever and whenever there was need. She would also be in touch with all the convents through her visits to the local houses and so, with her knowledge of the sisters, would be able to appoint sisters suitable for the work that had to be done. Above all, a Superior General would ensure that the active work of the sisters was based on a solid spiritual foundation. As Julie left the Bishop's presence she prayed for guidance. She believed that God wanted her sisters to work wherever there was a need but her belief conflicted with the Bishop's plans for Notre Dame, and Julie would never disobey the Bishop.

Not very long after this interview, Julie was asked to go to Bordeaux to talk to a community of sisters there about their Rule. Before she set out, Mgr Demandolx asked her to travel by way of Paris so that she could deliver letters from Father de Sambucy to Father Varin. Julie was delighted at the opportunity to see her old friend and spiritual director again for it was he who helped her to draw up the Rule which the sisters followed and she knew she could rely on his support over the question of having a Superior General.

Father Varin greeted her very warmly and after inquiring about her journey asked if she would mind waiting while he read the letters she had brought him. After reading them, he returned to Julie who was astonished at his anger when he spoke to her. The letters from Father de Sambucy repeated the accusation that had been made previously about Julie's so-called disobedience, jealousy and dictatorial manner. Father Varin told Julie that no Bishop wanted her in his Diocese and ordered her to return immediately to Amiens and beg Father de Sambucy to draw up the Rule and way of life for the sisters as he saw fit. Julie was upset and bewildered by the change in Father Varin's attitude towards her. She could hardly believe what she was hearing. Heartbroken she made her way back to the convent in Paris where she was staying and there in the chapel she prayed in sorrow as Our Lord did in Gethsemane: 'Not my will but thine be done.'

After Julie left him, Father Varin thought about his treatment of Julie and about her great humility and wrote a strongly worded letter to Father de Sambucy defending Julie and refuting all the charges that had been made against her. Julie made her way back to Amiens and went immediately to Father de Sambucy to ask him if he would draw up a new Holy Rule for the sisters. He agreed to do so and Julie continued on her way home.

Arriving back at her convent, Julie found the sisters in great distress. The Bishop had forbidden the entire community to receive Holy Communion for a period of time as a penance for what he considered their disobedience to his authority.

Julie made enquiries about the cause of this extreme punishment and was told that while she was in Paris, Victoire had reported to Father de Sambucy that the sisters had shown her a lack of respect. A few of the young sisters had laughed at something that had happened in the refectory and Victoire had taken their laughter as a personal insult. One good outcome of the young sisters' indiscretion was that Victoire did not return to the refectory again on the day she felt slighted and so Françoise was given the opportunity to talk freely to the sisters about the difficulty she and Julie were having with regard to their Rule.

She ended her talk by saying that if she and Julie were not accepted in Amiens they would go elsewhere and told the sisters that they would be free either to go with them or to remain behind. This was the first time mention had been made of leaving Amiens. The Sisters listened carefully to what Françoise had to say and then said unanimously that they too would go with Julie and Françoise.

It was probably this, rather than Victoire's hurt feelings, that brought down such a dreadful punishment on the sisters. They were told that a lack of respect to Victoire was an act of disobedience to the Bishop and were warned that if they were not careful they were in danger of committing mortal sin and earning eternal damnation.

Gradually peace was restored to the community and Julie continued to see Father de Sambucy about his revision of the Rule. Eventually, she was presented with a Rule taken from a congregation founded in the seventeenth century. This Rule did not in any way reflect the changes in society and spirituality that had happened since the seventeenth century. Julie and Françoise believed that it did not meet the needs of their time.

Julie asked for a longer period of time to consider the Rule she had been given but was refused. Once again she turned to God for enlightenment and asked some of the older sisters to join her in a novena of prayer to the Child Jesus. Their prayers were answered towards the end of the novena when a letter from the Bishop arrived informing her that unless Françoise settled all her income on the convent in Amiens, he would refuse to give them a Rule and a priest to say Mass in the convent. Françoise and Julie realised that if they agreed to his ultimatum, the other houses of Notre Dame would be cut off from the financial help they needed. Françoise told the Bishop she could not agree to this and on the following day Julie received a document from the Bishop telling her that she could leave Amiens and take with her the sisters who wished to go with her. He informed her that he would take back the convent in Amiens he had leased to her and would use it as a convent to form 'true sisters of Notre Dame'.

Prayer

Lord, you make all things new.
I pray for all those who are divided by anger
and mistrust, that they may grow together
in peace and love.

Gospel Reflection

Matthew 10:24, 25, 28

A pupil does not rank above his teacher, or a servant above his master. The pupil should be content to share his teacher's lot, the servant to share his master's. If the master has been called Beelzebub, how much more his household!

Do not fear those who kill the body, but cannot kill the soul. Fear him rather who is able to destroy both soul and body in hell.

Save me, Lord, from those intent on harming me
who plan to bring about my downfall.
Protect me from their anger and their evil deeds
and the poison of their words that seek to destroy me.
Their words are not to be trusted.
Protect me from their hypocrisy and evil schemes.
Do not let them triumph over me.

Lord, you hear the voices of the poor,
the homeless and oppressed.
Hear me now as I call on you in my need.
Let your truth and justice guide me so that
I may live for ever in your love.

Adapted from Psalm 139

Namur

Vindication

'I told you so, but you didn't listen.' The words rang out clearly in the tearoom and most of the people round about smiled because they were said by a pretty little girl of about 6 years of age and were spoken to an even younger child, probably her sister. I would love to have known what caused the reproach but had to hurry away to the bus station.

As the bus made its way through the streets, I thought of the two children and their words and came to the conclusion that 'I told you so' must be one of the hardest phrases in the English language *not* to say, and that there is really nothing to be gained by 'I told you so' – whoever the words are spoken to has already learned their mistake. Nor does the phrase do anything for the morale of the person to whom it is said: it merely confirms one's own sense of righteousness. And yet, how hard it is not to say it. Julie could have said these words time and again to the people who had opposed and misjudged her but instead she remained silent, following her rule of, 'Leave things to the good God'. After she died the Bishop of Namur said, 'Mère Julie will be canonised some day because during all her long trials at Amiens she never once failed in charity.'

Julie set out for Namur four days after her expulsion from Amiens to be joined two months later by Françoise and the rest of the sisters – all except Victoire and another sister who remained behind in Amiens.

The sisters soon settled in Namur and were fully occupied teaching the poor children who came to their school. Many of the parents who visited the school had very little religious knowledge and many of them had forgotten how to pray. Now they asked the sisters to teach them so that they too could pray with their children to the 'good God'. In the evenings, the sisters held classes in lace-making so that the young women who attended them would be able to earn a living. At the same time the sisters taught them about God's goodness and his great love for them. As the number of sisters grew, so did the number of pupils in the poor school. One well-meaning priest advised Julie to cut down on the number of these pupils so that she could make more room for paying boarders, but Julie would not hear of his suggestion: the children of the poor were her priority.

Meanwhile the convent in St Nicholas in Ghent was proving unsatisfactory both from a health point of view and from the hostility of the people who objected to French people working in their parish. Barely able to provide food and other necessities for themselves, the sisters' health began to deteriorate and Julie decided it was time to leave St Nicholas. She approached the recently appointed Bishop of Ghent, Mgr de Broglie, who agreed that the sisters should move elsewhere but asked that they should remain in his diocese. This was easier said than done. For four months the sisters searched for a house and during that time lived in extreme poverty trying to earn a living by making and selling lace. Eventually they managed to buy an old Cistercian abbey.

While Julie was busy helping the sisters in Ghent, Father de Sambucy was also busy writing letters to the Bishop of Ghent, blackening Julie's character and warning him against her. He even went so far as to offer to send sisters from Amiens to replace Julie and her sisters. Mgr de Broglie was furious at Father de Sambucy's attempt to interfere in the running of his diocese and was horrified to learn that, even before Julie had left Amiens, Father de Sambucy had for years been secretly training sisters in another congregation to replace her. He wrote to Father de Sambucy, accusing him of deceit and disloyalty to Julie and warned him against interfering in the affairs of his diocese.

Julie had one more meeting with Father de Sambucy. On the advice of Father Varin, Françoise had refused to leave all her finances with Father de Sambucy but now that she and Julie had been expelled from Amiens, they were advised to ask Father de Sambucy to return the money that belonged to them. On nine occasions Julie asked for the money to be given back but to no avail. Finally, under pressure from Father Varin and Father Thomas, Father de Sambucy agreed to return the money and Julie arranged to collect it. One can imagine how Julie felt when the sum of money was given to her not in notes but in coins. With great difficulty she struggled back to Namur weighed down with two heavy baskets of coins, terrified that she would be robbed on the way. Afterwards she laughed about her journey but said that at the time she was often very frightened.

Meanwhile in Amiens, Father de Sambucy's plan to establish a new community was failing badly. Lacking good leadership and, more important, without a sound spiritual formation, many of the sisters left the religious life. Unwilling to relinquish his ambition of directing a convent, Father de Sambucy wrote to Julie begging her to return as Superior to Amiens. Julie must have had a wry smile when she recieved this request and thought of all the times he had tried to drive her away from Amiens. She wrote to him in reply that as it was the Bishop who had expelled her only the Bishop could recall her. This was the last communication that Julie had with Father de

Sambucy for, unknown to her at the time, Father de Sambucy, not content with meddling in religious matters, was found by the authorities to be interfering in political affairs and was arrested. After his release he travelled to Rome where he once again began interfering in a religious congregation – this time the Congregation of the Sisters of the Sacred Heart. Whereas in Amiens his scheming went undetected, in Rome he was soon found out and obliged to return to France in disgrace.

At last Mgr Demandolx realised how Father de Sambucy had manipulated him and wrote to Julie asking her to return to Amiens. Julie replied, as she had so often told him before, that she could not confine herself to one diocese but would have to be free to oversee all the convents in her Congregation and be able to go wherever her sisters were needed. Within two weeks of receiving her letter the Bishop wrote to Julie again, assuring her that he regarded her as the Superior General of the Sisters of Notre Dame and stating that he had no intention of confining the sisters to his diocese. His letter ended with a plea for Julie to return to Amiens.

Not wanting to rush headlong into a situation that might prove impossible, Julie decided to visit Amiens and see for herself the state of affairs there. She discovered very quickly that the convent in Amiens had great debts and no means of paying them off and that the school had very few pupils – all boarders – who added to the burden of debt rather than decrease it. As for the sisters who were there, she saw that their spirit and way of life were in complete contrast to that of the sisters she had left behind in Belgium. Julie knew that the sisters in Amiens and the convents they had founded could never be part of her Congregation. She prayed for guidance because her decision was not an easy one to make. She was sorry at the thought of leaving Amiens; it was the first foundation she had made and had things worked out differently, it would have become the Mother House of the Congregation. She also felt sad at having to leave France which was, after all, her native land and where her family still lived. But Julie had given herself entirely to God to do whatever he wanted her to do and to go wherever he showed her the way. In her prayer she believed that Our Lord was telling her to leave Amiens and return to Namur which now became the Mother House of the Sisters of Notre Dame de Namur.

Prayer

Lord Jesus Christ, help me not to be critical
  or judgemental and especially, on the odd occasion
  when I am right, help me not to say, 'I told you so'.

Gospel Reflection

Matthew 18:21-22

Then Peter came up and asked him, 'Lord, how am I to forgive
my brother if he goes on wronging me? As many as seven
times?' Jesus replied, 'I do not say seven times; I say seventy
times seven.'

Here is my servant, whom I uphold,

my chosen one in whom I delight;

I have bestowed my spirit upon him

and he will make justice shine on the nations.

He will not call out or lift his voice high,

or make himself heard in the open street.

He will not break the bruised reed,

or snuff out a smouldering wick;

he will make justice shine on every race,

never faltering, never breaking down.

He will plant justice on earth,

while coasts and islands wait for his teaching.

Isaiah 42:1-4

Ghent

The Abbey Cat

The other day I reread the story told by Father De Mello about the Abbot's cat that used to wander into the Chapter room when the monks were in conference. The cat became as used to attending conferences as did the monks become used to the cat's presence. When the cat died, the monks found that they could no longer have conferences without the presence of a cat so they got another one. The story is amusing and I am sure untrue, but the point is that trivial things can assume gigantic proportions and that what has been accepted as custom can become rule.

Julie knew the difference well between what was important and what was not. She did not hang on to the past as unchangeable but neither did she seek changes that were unnecessary. She prayed for wisdom trusting that God would direct her in all the decisions she had to make. It was this openness to God's will that brought her at times into conflict with Church authorities and even with her own sisters.

It might have been thought that Julie's troubles were over when Notre Dame was settled in Belgium, but this was not the case. Napoleon, having conquered almost all of Europe, set about to 'reform' religious congregations according to his own ideas and once again the Congregation came under threat; not from the Church this time but from the Emperor himself. He thought it would be convenient to have two large groups of religious sisters – those who nursed and those who taught – instead of the many congregations that existed in the Empire. His was certainly a neat, military way of dealing with all the different Orders, but one that ignored their individual, spiritual charisms. Fortunately for Notre Dame and for all the other religious he never succeeded in carrying out this plan. He did, however, make a serious attempt to bring the Church in France completely under his control. After invading the Papal States and taking Pope Pius VII a prisoner to Fontainebleau, he ordered all the members of the hierarchy to acknowledge the right of France to be independent of the Pope in religious affairs. Many of the bishops, including the Bishop of Ghent, refused to agree to this and were banished from their dioceses.

Julie was very distressed to learn that Mgr Broglie, who was a great support to Notre Dame and who had become her personal friend, was among those who were imprisoned and exiled. She asked the sisters to pray constantly for him and for the Pope but, sadly, Julie was never to see Mgr Broglie again.

What caused Julie the greatest suffering of her life was that some of her sisters turned against her believing that she condoned Napoleon's attacks on the authority of the Pope. In a 'Universal Catechism' issued by Napoleon and ordered to be used throughout the Empire, the right of the Pope to intervene in the religious affairs of the Empire was denied, and any bishop refusing to adopt the catechism faced banishment from his diocese. The priests in Ghent noted that Bishop Pisani, the Bishop of Namur, had escaped exile and they presumed he must have accepted Napoleon's catechism. These priests had a very strong influence on the sisters in Ghent and warned them that Julie, who was a friend of Bishop Pisani, was in danger of leading not only Namur but also the whole Congregation into error. It was one of the saddest times in her life. Françoise wrote in her Memoirs that Julie wept to think that her sisters could believe her capable of such a betrayal of the Church and of the Pope.

In an attempt to clear Bishop Pisani's reputation, Julie

brought one of the sisters who had been most out-spoken against the Bishop to meet him so that she could hear for herself that he had never adopted the catechism. However, in spite of this, the sister was not convinced. What the sisters in Ghent were unaware of was that Bishop Pisani was an old friend of the Minister who had charge of implementing Napoleon's edict and because of this he was allowed to ignore Napoleon's decree. In fact, it was chiefly through Bishop Pisani's efforts that the government gave up the idea altogether of imposing the catechism on the whole of Belgium.

Perhaps the sisters in Ghent thought that Julie was too old to continue as Reverend Mother General or that they considered themselves to be more steadfast in their religious observances than Julie, for it was from Ghent that her final cross came. Julie had always a great liberty of spirit. It was this spirit that inspired her to found an order that would always be ready to meet the needs of the time. A simple example of how she practised this in small affairs was when she would suddenly interrupt the novices' lessons regardless of their timetable and send them out to weed or gather fruit. What was of importance to Julie was the daily living out of the Gospels in a spirit of simplicity, charity and obedience, not the day-to-day routine of life in a convent. When need arose, Julie would change the order of the day, omitting, if need be, what was not essential. The sisters in Ghent, however, lived according to a very structured way of life. The timetable that they had followed as young sisters in Namur was regarded as sacrosanct and they were horrified when they heard that Julie was not keeping to it rigorously in Namur. They had also begun to follow a rule of life from a sixteenth century religious order called the 'Institute of Mary'.

This rule had been recommended to the sisters merely as a spiritual reading book and was never intended to become the rule for Notre Dame. They, however, regarded this rule as binding and complained, first of all among themselves and then openly to priests whom they knew, that Julie was breaking the 'rule'. Things became so bad that there was almost a division in the Congregation between those who followed Julie and those who followed the rule of the Institute of Mary. Finally, at Julie's request, Bishop Pisani appointed an ecclesiastical superior who helped to resolve the conflict in the Congregation, making clear what was of rule and what was a matter of daily, routine practice. Throughout this time of opposition Julie felt great sorrow but not resentment or anger. When others spoke to her about her critics, she excused them saying that they meant well. According to Françoise, the only thing that disturbed Julie in the midst of all this trial was how it affected God's cause.

Prayer

Lord, give me the grace to see things as you see them
    so that I may be able to distingush between what is
    important and what is worthless.
Help me to be true to your teaching
    and to change whatever in my life
    needs changing.

Gospel Reflection

Mark 7:5-10

Accordingly, these Pharisees and the lawyers asked him, 'Why
do your disciples not conform to the ancient tradition, but eat
their food with defiled hands?' He answered, 'Isaiah was right
when he prophesied about you hypocrites in these words:
"This people pays me lip-service, but their heart is far from
me: their worship of me is in vain, for they teach as doctrines
the commandments of men." You neglect the commandment
of God, in order to maintain the tradition of men.'

Despatch her (Wisdom) from the holy heavens,
send her forth from your throne of glory
to help me and to toil with me
and teach me what is pleasing to you,
since she knows and understands everything.
She will guide me prudently in my undertakings
and protect me by her glory.
Then all I do will be acceptable.

Wisdom 9:10-12

Namur

Into the Light

The newspaper headlines mourned the loss of farmers' livelihoods as disease swept through their livestock. The country was horror-stricken as more and more cattle and flocks were killed. Farmers were quoted as saying it was as if they experienced death themselves because the future held no hope for them and their families, and some thought it would be better to commit suicide than face the uncertain future.

Every day we read or hear about people who experience a kind of death in their lives: workers who are suddenly made unemployed; parents whose children reject them; married couples who separate – the list could go on and on. To a lesser extent every one of us has known a kind of death in our own lives, not just the physical death of someone we love but a personal death when we have been ignored or passed over for someone else, or have been judged unjustly. If we have been deeply wounded something in us seems to die. Jesus, too, knew these deaths in his life and in the end experienced the physical death of dying in agony on the Cross.

In her life Julie was rarely without suffering but accepted it as coming from God and as a means of becoming more like Christ. As she wrote to her sisters, 'There must be a little cross everywhere. Let us follow after our good Jesus by carrying it.'

Julie's one aim in life was to bring others to love the good God and it was for this that she spent herself tirelessly in God's service. Her many journeys and the mental and physical suffering she endured gradually began to tell upon her health. She felt her strength declining and knew that God would soon be calling her to be with him for ever. In a letter to the Superior of Jumet she wrote, 'I am growing so old. Every day I fear to be suddenly overtaken by death. I go on as if I were 20, but that will pass like many other things . . . A short time hence and we shall no longer be. Let us work at bearing fruit worthy of eternal life!'

On 14 January 1816, at the age of 64, Julie injured herself badly when she fell on the stairs in the convent. She was carried to her room to be nursed and remained there for a while until she was able to move about again. Although well looked after, she began to suffer continuously from headaches and colds and found moving painful and eating almost impossible.

What made matters worse was that it was at this time that the sisters in Ghent were complaining about what they thought was Julie's laxity regarding the Rule and about the bad influence they thought Mgr Pisani had on her. Françoise was ill at this time too, but when she was able to visit Julie she used to read passages that Julie was particularly fond of from *The Imitation of Christ*. One passage Julie liked to hear was, 'If you carry the cross of Jesus, it will carry you and will lead you to the longed-for goal where you will find an end to sufferings which in this life have no end.'

Julie's illness lasted almost four months. On the evening of Palm Sunday, her condition became much worse and the sisters gathered to kneel in prayer at her bedside. As they knelt there, they heard a gentle voice quietly singing the Magnificat.

Julie's last words were a hymn of praise to her good God for all the graces he had given her throughout her life. She never spoke again. On the next day, 8 April, Julie gave up her soul to God. Françoise, who had visited her on Palm Sunday was, sadly, not well enough to be at Julie's bedside when she died.

Julie had requested that her funeral should be a simple one, but the Bishop insisted on a solemn ceremony that was attended by a huge congregation of people who were convinced that they were attending the funeral of a saint.

People began praying to Julie to intercede for them with God and through her intercession many were cured miraculously. On 13 May 1906, Julie was beatified by Pope Pius X and in 1969 was declared a saint by Pope Paul VI.

Prayer

Lord, comfort and console all
    who are suffering pain
    of mind or body.
Give your peace to those
    who are dying and let them
    feel your love as they journey
    from this world to be with you
    in everlasting life.

Scripture Reflection

Romans 6:3-5

Have you forgotten that when we were baptised into union with Christ Jesus we were baptised into his death? By baptism we were buried with him and lay dead, in order that, as Christ was raised from the dead in the splendour of the Father, so also we might set our feet upon the new path of life. For if we have become incorporate with him in death like his, we shall also be one with him in resurrection like his.

Lord, I praise your infinite wisdom.
Your words are my guide by day.
At night I ponder on their meaning,
keeping them close to my heart.
I have no fear for
your words are my strength.
They promise me life everlasting.

Even though my body should die,
you have conquered death and
you will bring me into everlasting life
where I shall rejoice for ever in your infinite goodness.

Adapted from Psalm 15

The Sisters of Notre Dame de Namur

Since St Julie's time the apostolate of the Sisters of Notre Dame has spread to five continents and has adapted to meet the needs of different cultures and different times.

Essentially the mission is as it was in Julie's day – to help the poor and the most abandoned. Nowadays this may mean teaching basic skills of literacy to the uneducated or it may mean helping the educated to work for justice and peace.

Today, the sisters work in Congo-Kinshasa, Kenya, Nigeria and Southern Africa, Japan, Britain, Italy, Belgium, Brazil, Peru, and the United States of America. Wherever they are their aim is to make God's goodness known to the world.

Ah, qu'il est bon, le bon Dieu!

Prayer to St Julie

Dear St Julie,
  God blessed you with humility and wisdom
  in the midst of struggle and misunderstanding.
Through you many came to know God's love
  and concern.
Through your intercession,
  may all threatened by revolutions and political unrest
  know the peace the world cannot give.
Through your intercession,
  may all those who are injured and physically disabled
  receive courage.
Through your intercession,
  may all who suffer misunderstanding
  as they follow the guidance of the Spirit
  know comfort.
Help us all to use our gifts of nature and grace
  for God's glory.
We ask this in the name of Jesus and his mother, Mary.

Amen.